The Little Book
of Big Frontiers

The Little Book of Big Frontiers

Rediscovering the Lost Realms of Christianity

John E. Worgul

WIPF *&* STOCK · Eugene, Oregon

THE LITTLE BOOK OF BIG FRONTIERS
Rediscovering the Lost Realms of Christianity

Wipf & Stock
An imprint of Wipf and Stock Publishers
199 W. 8th Ave., Suite 3
Eugene, OR 97401

www.wipfandstock.com

ISBN 13: 978-1-62032-160-7

Manufactured in the U.S.A.

To my wife, Kathy Anne,
a true disciple of Jesus

Contents

Acknowledgments

I WOULD NOT HAVE written this book were it not for the persistent encouragement of my friend and student, Dr. David Waters, to put into writing the ideas on cosmology I had formulated in class over the years. David also directed me to Peter Kreeft's book *Love is Stronger than Death*, which was very helpful in formulating the last chapter. I am thankful for my friends Paula Niederberger, Rev. Jason Poling, Diane Steenburg, and Fr. Lawrence Weinholt, for reading and correcting the manuscript. The imperfections, of course, are all mine.

Introduction

The Water Bugs

ON A CHILLY DECEMBER evening in 1977, I first noticed the water bugs. While sitting on a low bridge over a small stream, there was just enough light in the starry sky to make out small objects bobbing and skipping upon the surface against the slow current. Curious, I bent over for a closer look. They were bugs with long legs whose feet made what looked to be little indentations on the cold winter water. It boggled my mind that bugs could be out on a December evening, let alone on the stream's frigid surface.

To this day I know nothing about them, not even what they are called. However, the bugs got me to thinking. For all appearances, these insects had no conception of what was underneath them. They lived on the surface. There was, at least in proportion to their tiny size, a whole watery world beneath them, to which they were connected but were unable to comprehend. The bugs seemed oblivious to this reality. Who knows what dangers lurked for them, or what delights to enjoy, just below the surface?

As I pondered this, it dawned on me that I was not altogether unlike the water bug. I too lived on the surface. At that time I was in seminary and had given my life over to the study of the deep things of God. Moreover, vivid life-changing encounters with God deeply moved and motivated me. However for all my study and experience of God, I was haunted with a growing realization that I was still a surface dweller. I could not get to where my soul longed to go. I was a tiny little water bug bobbing upon the surface; beneath and above and all around there was a far greater reality I intuitively knew was there but could not grasp.

This thought has followed me ever since. I think there will always be the water bug in me, because there will always be a sense of living on the surface before the sheer vastness of the regions surrounding me and, indeed, within me. Water bugs are humble creatures, and so should we be. Yet, we are more than a bug. The water bug goes about its short life with neither hopes nor dreams nor remorse. It lives purely by instinct. It is programmed to do some marvelous things like bobbing upon the water, surviving in the cold, hunting for whatever it is that it eats, and procreating in a hostile environment. It knows no moral failure, has no expectations, and does not have choices to make. It is locked in its own little world, and to this the bug is absolutely suited. By merely existing, it performs what is expected of it.

Such bliss is not ours. Even the most complacent souls have at least some vague sense of the frontiers beyond their front doors. We can lock these vistas out but not without great loss to our humanity. We may look through our windows from time to time and notice distant horizons, but most of us are overcome by the sheer magnitude of these frontiers and recede back into our comfortable habits of being. We might even get excited about the fact that there are unexplored regions beyond our boredom and mediocrity, but in the end we never set out to explore for one reason or another, usually fear.

The frontiers that are before us are both near and far, within and without, and they are all interconnected. As the word "frontiers" suggests, they are wild and fraught with the unexpected, yes, even danger. Each one is vast; there is no clear end to them nor boundaries, like, for instance, the Pacific Ocean was for the early American pioneers. To begin with, there is the frontier within each of us, a vast expanse of spiritual space, and a universe in miniature. It is a dimension that very much mirrors the world about us, full of beauty yet permeated with corruption. Dangers lurk within, but there is also life, power, and potential. To most of us, this frontier remains largely unexplored. Yet we are bidden to take the journey within. Why should we even venture on such a journey? How do we do this? What will we find?

There is also the vast frontier of spiritual space outside of us called the "heavens" in the Bible. It is populated with angels of all sorts as well as with the immortal souls who have passed on into it through death. It is a place of order, beauty, and rest. Yet, there are elements of craziness, chaos, and the din of demons intent on our very destruction. How real is this realm to us? How does this frontier intersect with our lives as we live them day by day?

Then there is the physical world around us. This globe is beautiful and inviting, yet ugly and terrifying as well. Before our senses lays a frontier beaming with mystery! Do we even see it? How do we live with the goodness around us and really enjoy it as it ought to be enjoyed? There is also the vast frontier of evil and suffering. Yes! It is real and part of the very fabric of our lives! Do we hide from it, or do we bravely face it and even entertain the thought that it is indeed a frontier to be explored? Finally, there is death itself, the final frontier. Should we live in dread of the inevitable? Can we even consider death to be a frontier to be explored here and now in a healthy way? What is beyond death's doors?

Overwhelming, isn't it? At this point we might think it easier to play the water bug and live on the surface. Somehow it seems safer there. This is an illusion; we cannot hide from these frontiers that press in on us. In fact, it is unnatural not to be curious about them. God has endowed each of us with powers to explore, to be pioneers of the whole of reality that is around us. Like today's computers, we possess within us a powerful search engine that is constantly roaming for information. By nature we want to know about things above and below, within and without. Moreover, we possess an acute power of longing and desire that drives us to seek freedom from fear and fulfillment of soul and body. We are also fighters; we will claw and scratch our way through thick and thin to get what we want and, indeed, our rightful destiny. We must attribute these strange and wonderful features to our Creator who endowed us with them. Indeed, in some mysterious way, tiny as we are in the scope of things, we are not bugs on the surface but divine image bearers gazing into the surface of a pool; one sees oneself, but one also sees God.

1

The Map Room

A Tale of a Lost Treasure Map: *I heard this story from a reliable source and have every reason to believe it. It is said that a pirate was caught by the British in colonial times and was brought to trial in London. He had done what many pirates did in those days. He stashed his ill-gotten gains in a certain place and made a map of where he placed them so he could protect them from his untrustworthy comrades and come back later to claim them. In this case the treasure was buried somewhere on the Delaware coast. When he was captured, the pirate gave the map to his lawyer and hoped that he could bargain with the British authorities—the map and the treasure for his life. As it turned out, the British wanted to make an example of him and hanged him. Evidently, the lawyer placed the map on top of a very heavy file cabinet, behind which it inadvertently fell. There it lay unfound and forgotten many years until its relatively recent discovery. It is rumored that the map is now in possession of someone in the United States who is tracking down this treasure.*

WHETHER YOU BELIEVE THIS story or not, one thing is clear: you would like to be in possession of such a map if it existed, and such maps must exist. Treasure and maps capture everyone's imagination. How can we explain this universal fascination with treasure maps? It must be that they represent a fundamental longing of the human soul for adventure, discovery, and precious things. We were made for discovery, and the excitement of adventure can be a holy passion. We here use the idea of a map to draw on our natural God-given curiosity. The concepts here may be a bit strange and hard to grasp at first, but every person who sets out on a quest must set his or her whole mind to the task, believing that the effort will be well worthwhile in the end.

Maps and frontiers go together. Pioneers make maps of regions hitherto unknown, and these become useful, even critical, for those who follow them. So, too, we have a map, but considering the nature of the frontiers we are investigating in this book, our map has to be rather unusual.

Let us use our imaginations and enter into a magnificent map room, lined with bookcases filled with leather-bound tomes of various shapes and sizes, a globe, microscopes, a telescope, and a domed ceiling that opens up to the sky. What grabs our attention, however, is a map spread out on a table in the middle of the room. At once we realize this is no ordinary map. First of all, the map is lit with a beam of light that ascends from its surface, straight up through the opening in the ceiling into the night sky. Indeed, we crane our necks and surmise that this beam keeps going on and on, and somehow we intuitively sense that it goes past the sun, moon, and planets of our solar system, all the way beyond the Milky Way and galaxies, in short, beyond creation.

The beam of this map points us to the first and ultimate frontier. This frontier is God himself. Scripture tells us that God is above the heavens and the earth. By "heavens" the Bible means both the physical heavens that we gaze out upon and the spiritual heavens that we understand as the supernatural realm that surrounds us. In both senses of the word God does not literally live in the "heavens," for even the heavens cannot contain him. This means that God is beyond anything we can comprehend. In fact, there really isn't anything we can think or say about God that can adequately express who he is. The thoughts by which we arrange our words to describe and communicate are not large enough to grasp God.

We might here ask, how can God be a frontier for us, since he is infinitely beyond us and we cannot even begin to map him out? Ah, but the beam from the map points upward and has got our attention. As we gaze upward, we come to a wonderful realization. Though we know that the Bible tells us God is like many things, such as light, an immovable rock, a father, or even a mother hen, he is beyond these things, even to the point that these images fail in the end to do God justice. We therefore make our way into the divine frontier by a sort of "yes and no" fashion. Yes, God is like many wonderful things we see and noble thoughts we think. However, ultimate knowledge of God comes when we gaze upward and realize—no, he is far beyond what we have experienced as earthly light or even a good father. When we realize this, we gain a spiritual knowledge that is beyond all earthly knowledge, one of inexpressible joy and full of glory. This is the realm of God who is above all human concept; we can only worship that which we cannot fully comprehend.

And so it is, the deeper we travel into this ultimate frontier, and the closer we get to God, the greater and more mysterious God becomes. This is a strange process, for we come to know by unlearning everything that we thought was accurate and sufficiently true. Moreover, moving into this divine frontier doesn't just happen; it takes a lifetime of journeying and working our way through other frontiers that we will discuss in this book. Still, we introduce it first, for we need to know the ultimate frontier for which our longing souls must aspire in order to be happy.

Now let us take another look at this map. It is a map of our world. We said that it was unusual, and indeed it is, for when we stare at any location, we see that it is alive with all the life we experience as we know it now. It has oceans, mountains, valleys, trees, towns, cities, and people. Now we might wonder how we might call this old earth a frontier, for it has grown small of late, and so much of it has been explored. Moreover, everything is so familiar to us; it is as if we have seen everything, if not in person, then through the media. When the things around us become so familiar in the hustle and bustle of our lives, they somehow become less real. We don't see, for instance, a tree as it really is, but as a green thing we have seen a hundred times before. On the other hand, when we hold material things as if they were ultimate, which is called idolatry, they always have a way of letting us down. When this happens, we become disappointed and jaded, and again they become less real to us.

This is where our map helps us; it reveals the beings and things of earth as they really are, not as we think they are. In this way, our world as we live in it here and now truly can become for us a new frontier. Our spiritual pilgrimage is very physical, indeed, for it begins with the glory God packed into everything around us, making our material world important and real to us as physical beings. Although God is completely beyond the universe, he also completely fills it with himself. Moreover, the incarnation of Jesus in flesh—just like ours—and his journey into our world of space and matter places the divine stamp of approval on creation. This is true in spite of this world's obvious drawbacks. Jesus invites us to see all the things of this world as a wonderful and amazing frontier. We will expand on this later.

Another feature of our map is most interesting. If we gaze at any one place on it, the history of that place unfolds before our eyes; indeed, the future of it is revealed as well. This feature has profound implications. Everything that has happened or will happen in time is stored away, not like digital photos on a microchip, but, rather, it is as if every moment there ever was still exists and never ceases to exist and is never lost. All beautiful moments always abide, all bitter moments linger with the hope of somehow sweetening, and all sins exist before God the judge. This means that time has purpose and is moving toward a goal. Scripture reveals to us that God has entered into time in various ways but most remarkably in Christ's incarnation, thus making time holy and full of potential, even a frontier to be explored.

How can time be a frontier? God has given us certain powers within the very depths of our being that we can utilize to explore it. The first is memory, through which we can experience the past even though we were not present. Hence the command by God for the celebration of the Passover for all generations of Israelites; their annual reenactment of that event binds them to that first Passover and the salvation at the Red Sea. All subsequent generations of Israel experienced it together as if they were originally there. Our Lord's command to "do this in remembrance of me" likewise brings all the church, past, present, and future, together before the very cross of Christ. The second power with which we are endowed is hope. Hope, informed by Scripture and guided by the Holy Spirit, transports us into the future kingdom in such a way that we can really see it. Finally, we have the imagination to energize memory and hope so that we can genuinely live in the past, present, and future. With these God-given powers we are expected to make the journey into time, to become "time-travelers," so to speak, in the frontier of time.

These three frontiers—God himself who is infinitely beyond us, yet borders on our territory, the realm of space and matter where we live, and the frontier of time—are very important for us to be aware of. If we do not intentionally journey into all three of them, our world begins to fall apart. What often happens is that one of these three will become real at the expense of one or both of the others. For instance, there are many who affirm a profound concept of God as being above and beyond us (like Eastern religions such as Buddhism and Islam) but who have little appreciation for the reality of space and matter. For the Buddhist, salvation is a sort of "beam me up, Scotty," a desire to escape into nirvana, for things are hopeless down here. For some Muslims it seems natural and appropriate, for instance, to strap bombs on their persons to blow themselves and others up and consider it to be a service to Allah. When the human soul connects with the idea of the eternal, it can be very intoxicating, for good or for bad.

On the other hand, there are those who have little or no appreciation for a God who stands above and beyond the universe, and therefore they embrace the material as all there is. When this happens, the world gradually loses all its meaning, for it has broken away from its spiritual anchor, and despair settles in. Finally, it is very common for folks to be deeply saddened by or afraid of time. Time brings change and deterioration; is viewed as an enemy and is seen as senseless, with no purpose. Or, we might indulge ourselves in the hope that time will bring us the "American dream" if we are capitalistic, or a communistic ideal society if Marxist, but it seems of late that humanity is losing faith in these fantasies. We no longer know what to think about time nowadays.

As we consider our unusual map, we begin to understand that as fantastic as it may seem to us at first, it really isn't all that outlandish. It speaks to our hearts and to the reality of our situation. Somewhere deep within the human soul we have a longing to reach out to a God who is above and beyond us, one whom we can never get enough of, one who will forever surprise us, and one who is worthy of our worship. Yet we also know that the material world around us, in spite of its deficiencies, is not an illusion, but real and, in the end, redeemable. Likewise, time is meaningful, it's going somewhere, and it has purpose. We need to venture in and totally immerse ourselves into all three frontiers simultaneously. These three features of our map provide the "lay of the land," so to speak, for the other frontiers that are before us in this book.

2

The Telescope, the Microscope, and the Hourglass

Meister Eckhart's Parable: *There was a learned man who, for eight years, desired that God would show him a man who would teach him the truth. And once when he felt a very great longing, a voice from God came to him and said, "Go to church, and there you will find a man who will show you the way to blessedness." He went there and found a poor man whose feet were torn and covered with dust and dirt, and all his clothing were but rags. He greeted him, saying—*

"God give you a good day!"

He answered, "I never had a bad day."

"God give you good luck."

"I never had bad luck."

"May you be happy! But why do you answer me like this?"

"I have never been unhappy."

"Please, explain this to me, for I cannot understand it."

The poor man answered, "Willingly. You wished me a good day; I never had a bad day. If I am hungry I praise God. If it freezes, hails, snows, rains, if the weather is fair or foul, still I praise God. When wretched and despised, I praise God, and so I have never had an evil day. You wished me that God would send me luck, but I never had bad luck, for I know how to live with God, and I know that what God gives me or ordains for me, be it good or bad I take it cheerfully from God as the best that can be, and so I never had bad luck. You wished that God would make me happy. I was never unhappy, for my only desire is to live in God's will, and I have so entirely yielded my will to God's that what God wills, I will."

"But if God should will to cast you into hell," said the learned man, "what would you do then?"

"Cast me into hell? His goodness forbids it! But if He did cast me into hell, I should have two arms to embrace Him. One arm is true humility that I should lay beneath Him, and thereby be united to His holy humanity. With the right arm of love, which is united with His holy divinity, I should so embrace Him that He would have to go to hell with me. I would rather be in hell and have God, than in heaven and not have God."

Then the learned man understood that true abandonment with utter humility is the nearest way to God.

He asked him further, "From where have you come?"

"From God."

"Where did you find God?"

"When I forsook all earthly things."

"Where have you left God?"

"In pure hearts, and in men of good will."

The learned man asked, "What sort of man are you?"

"I am a king."

"Where is your kingdom?"

"My soul is my kingdom, and this kingdom is greater

than any kingdom on earth."

MUCH COULD BE SAID of this parable, but in this chapter we are going to explore the last grand line "My soul is my kingdom, and this kingdom is greater than any kingdom on earth." Yes, there is a vast frontier within all of us, a "spiritual space," a kingdom if you will, just waiting for us to discover.

You might remember the map room we were just in was furnished with a telescope. I have always been intrigued with telescopes. Back in grade school a fellow student brought one to school for show and tell. It didn't work, but he knew I was interested in it and wanted to trade it for my old radio which did not work either. The day was overcast and snowy, yet he confidently pointed the scope up in the sky and urged me to look through it. As I gazed into the gray, I exclaimed that I thought I saw a snowflake. He knowingly smiled in encouragement, and the deal was made. It turned out that I never progressed in astronomy much beyond this broken telescope, but the fascination has always been there.

In spite of this, I am aware that since Galileo's invention modern man has become ever more impressed with the sheer magnitude of the universe. We have all heard statistics. The Milky Way, just one galaxy among a countless host, would take 100,000 years to traverse if moving at the speed of light. By analogy, if our solar system were the size of a quarter, the Milky Way would span an area the size of the US! The telescopes we now have search ever deeper into space; it is amazing how it all widens out from the mere lens attached to a tube!

The microscope tells the other side of the story. We look down, and to our eyes everything close up seems small and manageable, at least in comparison to the universe above. Yet we know this is not true. Around and about us spreads a vast web of tiny cell life, and beyond that, vast regions of atomic reality, virtual galaxies comparable to the heavens above in ratio of size to distance. It is striking to contemplate that electrons swirl around the atomic nucleus much like planets spin around the sun. We will never succeed in actually seeing this, however powerful our microscopes may become, because the light required to peer into the mysteries of the atom would alter the structure of the atom in view. The realm of the small is as vast as the realm of the large.

Now imagine a man in our map room. He looks up through his telescope, and the heavens open up to him like a cone expanding from the lens of the scope. He then looks down through his microscope, and the microscopic world opens up to him like a cone expanding from the lens of his scope. He stands at the very point where both cones come together in the map room, standing, as it were, at the narrow passageway of an hourglass, at the very center where these vast frontiers merge. Astronomers, quick to ridicule the old idea that the earth is the center of the universe, love to point out that the earth is not the center of our solar system, nor is our solar system in the middle of our galaxy, nor is our galaxy the middle of our universe. Be this as it may, it is clear that we stand at the center between the universe of the very large above and the universe of the very small below. Moreover, we are very conscious of both and are equipped with an intelligence that can search out and contemplate them.

Let us go one step further with our idea of the hourglass. Imagine that the complete physical world, both the large and the small, in one unified whole, stands above each one of us like the top cone of the hourglass. Then, let us look within ourselves as spiritual beings. In the same way the microscope opens up an entire "mini" universe unseen to the human eye, we too have an interior spiritual universe opening up like an expanding cone within us, unseen to the human eye, comparable to the physical universe above and about us. Again, our eyes cannot see it, but our eyes cannot see the atom either. We know the atom is there because the atomic theory answers certain questions we raise about the nature and behavior of the physical world. Likewise, we know there is something that we might call "spiritual space" within, because this concept answers certain questions we raise about the nature and behavior of the human being.

Our concept of the hourglass places us, therefore, not only at the point of contact between the universe above and the universe below, but also at the central channel connecting the vast realms of the physical universe outside and the spiritual universe within. Two biblical images describe the reality and immensity of the spiritual space within each of us. The first is that we are the temple of God. When we moderns think of a temple, we think of a mere building for worship. When the ancients thought of a temple, they considered it a representation of the universe in miniature. For instance, the "bronze sea" containing water for ritual cleansing in Solomon's Temple is called a "sea" because it represents the watery deep upon which God founded the earth. The freestanding pillars at the entrance, named Yakin (He will establish) and Boaz (in strength), represent the mountains, the pillars upon which the sky rests. The "mercy seat" in the Most Holy Place is the very point where God, who is beyond all creation, actually touches this created world. The temple was the center of the earth but also represented the world as it should be, rightly ordered.

To understand ourselves as temples as the ancients understood temples, we have to see ourselves as a universe in miniature. God inhabits space, particularly sacred space, but also inhabits what we here call "spiritual space." God fills the universe, but he fills the temple in particular. There is a vastness within of which we must be aware to understand ourselves correctly. This brings us to the second image the Bible uses to awaken us to the reality of spiritual space. Christ himself tells us that the kingdom of heaven is within us. Unless we are willing to dismiss his words as merely symbolic, at best a thought-provoking idea, we have to understand this in terms of real spiritual space. A kingdom is vast and glorious. There must be something large enough within us to contain God. God, who dwells in us, is not cramped in close quarters.

Let us return to our discussion in the previous chapter concerning the powers of the soul to illustrate this point from our own experience. We close our eyes, and by means of our memory and imagination we can summon up an image of just about any place we have been. We can go to the beach; we see the waves, hear the pounding surf, the screeching of seagulls, and feel and sniff the salty air. Our eyes scan miles and miles to the horizon. We can go to the mountains, intuit the ancient quality of rocky clefts, survey steep canyon walls, kick stones down into the ravine, and break out of a pine forest into sudden view of a valley so vast and still we are stunned by its silence. For that matter, we can go to places where we haven't even been by the mere act of imagining, by taking scraps of images stored in our minds or felt in our souls, and putting them together to form an imaginary world. How can we experience such large tracks of space and matter, such lively imagery as if we are actually present, and move back in time with such ease, all from within?

Of course one may reduce this phenomenon of memory and imagination down to mere neurological functions. However, Scripture and church teaching over the centuries inform us that this power is attributed to our having been created in the image of God. We were made with a spiritual dimension that mirrors creation, an internal universe that reflects images born in the eternal mind of God. To pull memories and images out of the treasury of our mind is nothing short of a divine-like quality.

We have all but lost this knowledge of spiritual space in our culture. To lose it is to become ignorant of the most precious part of us, in fact, the very interior core of our being. We therefore approach our "spiritual space" as a frontier, an expansive territory that must be explored so as to truly know ourselves. As we shall see, this sets us on an adventure that is both thrilling and terrifying.

> Understand that you are another world in miniature and that there is within you the sun, the moon, and the stars.
>
> —Origen, *Homilies on Leviticus*, Homily 5.

3

The Cathedral

I will never forget that bright June morning in 1975 when I saw my first cathedral. Our summer missions group arrived in Amiens, France, late the night before and settled in at a hostel. Hostels, of course, are not noted for comfort, so after a weary trip and a restless night, I was anxious to get up and take in my first impressions of France, in particular, a cathedral. As I remember it, we were a few miles away, and the famous cathedral looked like a box from that distance. With excitement we headed for it, walking along ancient French streets that, for an American Midwesterner twenty years of age, radiated a charm that would never be forgotten.

The cathedral itself became hidden from our view by the houses and buildings we were passing. Suddenly, we emerged into an open space where the huge edifice burst into full view. Immediately I was rocked with astonishment at the great, wild Gothic before me. The flying buttresses and wonderful stonework exuded a quality of age I had never seen before; timeworn statuary commemorated great men of hoary antiquity. Upon entering, our heads were automatically drawn

*upwards, following the great pillars of the nave
unique to this particular church.*

THE THIRTEENTH-CENTURY BUILDERS NOT only looked upward as they raised stone upon stone to the lofty vaulted heights, but they also looked inward to their souls. The reality of interior spiritual space was common knowledge to the people of this age. They understood that as they were building their great church they were also building a cathedral within. Their church told a story in stone, wood, and glass—the story of creation and redemption. The very columns and vaulting were inspired by the great trees of northern Europe, God's cathedral of nature. Like nesting dolls, the cathedral was a mini-world and the soul another world within a world. When the satisfied builders gazed down the aisle to the great altar, lit with the most colorful beams of light, they were gazing into their own souls.

Strange as it might seem to most of us, the soul has architecture; it is not without structure. This structure is a mirror of creation. God made Adam and Eve to fit their environment; both physically and spiritually they matched it. The outside has much to reveal about the inside, and the inside has something to reveal about the outside. To explore the outside is to explore the inside. With our science we cannot penetrate all the secrets of creation; the more we learn, the more mysterious our universe becomes. Likewise, one can be a student of a particular cathedral for a lifetime and still discover new things. The same is true about the soul. Thus the human soul can rightly be understood as a frontier—a frontier of the interior.

We can press this analogy even further. Amiens Cathedral today is a mere ghost of a place compared to what it was when first built. The original builders would hardly recognize it now. I spent the whole day there back in June of 1975. As far as I could tell, hardly anyone worshipped there. The place had the feel of a long-aged sleep. The cavernous transepts and choir were dark, gray, and damp. In fact, I remember a bat flying overhead, suggesting to my mind a hint of Gothic horror. None of the original stained glass was in place; all that met the eye was clear glass. Its famous choir stalls featuring a wood carving of the whole Bible still braved the passage of time, but all I can remember of it is Job and his artfully carved boils!

When the church was pristine, even the stones of the front façade were painted in striking colors. The cathedral had been the very center of the community, vibrant with sound and color, pulsating with life. You see, the edifice reflected the interior, the very souls of those who created it. Likewise, today the building reflects the spiritual condition of those outside and around it. We might even say that the cathedral represents a "fall" from grace. It still is a church, made in the "image" of its creators, but it is a mere shadow of what it was.

Amiens Cathedral as it stands today provides an analogy for this natural world on one hand and natural humanity on the other. As for this natural world, we know that in spite of all its wonder, it is not what it was originally and not what it is supposed to be. The same can be said of natural humanity; we are as complex as nature is around us, structured and beautiful on the one hand but wild and dark on the other. We may even go so far as to say that each of us has a "crypt" like the old church, somewhat like an underworld, a dark place that we vaguely know is there, a "frontier" in the depths left largely unexplored. We all have some light high up in the church above corresponding to the light of this world's sky, but we all have a crypt way down deep in the vaults below, a virtual hell. We are like Amiens Cathedral, and the cathedral is like the world around it, like nesting dolls that fit together.

We must deeply respect every human being before us. Each person we see is a world in miniature, a cathedral, though bereft of its original glory, still reflecting the image of his or her creator. Each person is engaged in his or her own personal struggle within his or her soul between the light of truth that still lingers in the old sanctuary above and dark forces of self destruction that lurk in the crypt below. It is true that each person is helpless to become what he or she must be for the glory of God to fill the whole edifice again; this takes a divine act of grace. Baldly speaking, we are corrupt and evil. However, the most essential truth about every human being is that we are divine image-bearers, cathedrals made for divine indwelling. When we look into a human face, we are looking into the façade of a cathedral, into the face of God.

A Christian is one who, by God's grace, has opened up the front portals of his or her soul to God, and is indwelt by Jesus through the work of the Holy Spirit. Christ begins the rebuilding of the sanctuary. The scaffolding is up, the masonry being repaired, glass of rich and brilliant colors being placed, rusty iron polished, organ pipes restored, and new paint applied. We are a cathedral in process of being renewed, conforming to the glory of the original world for which we were made. Our souls are a vast and spacious sanctuary where Christ is enthroned on the altar within. We become increasingly familiar with our spiritual space and, with some encouragement, will set upon the exploration of our interior frontier, the universe within.

How strange and wonderfully made we are! We could see the whole universe through a single person if we had the eyes to see it. Within each of us is something like a sky that symbolizes the lofty heights of light, spiritual aspirations, and creativity. Within each of us is something like this earth with all of its rich soil, gardens, mountains, and seas, as well as deserts, weeds, and noxious things. Indeed, we even have an underworld, a place of hidden terror, of unbounded evil, and speaking metaphorically, the abode of a dragon in the cavernous depths below. This dark region will be explored in another chapter, but first we will expand our concept of the world around us.

4

The Pie

I am a native of Michigan, and Michigan means, among other things, an abundance of fruit. The climate of the Great Lakes area is perfect for orchards and vineyards, and in my experience, the growing of cherries in particular. Our family would occasionally visit the northwestern shore of Lake Michigan for vacations, and if the time was right, we picked our fill of bright red, sour cherries. I remember getting a stomachache after gorging myself.

One of my fondest memories is of the pies my mother made with these cherries. I love pies. In fact, I even love the sound of the word "pie." Apart from their tasty sweetness and scrumptious crusts, pies are perfect not only as a dessert but also in their geometric shape, the perfection of the circle. I therefore have a personal preference in using the pie as a way to visualize creation in all of its glory.

LET US LOOK AT all creation as a very large pie. Then, imagine that every single part of creation, whether a bird, tree, mountain, or whatever, is a piece of this pie. Each is a part of the whole, and this means everything has its place in creation. Now this may sound very simple, but it is indeed a very important point. Everything around us is either created by God or fashioned by humans who can create and invent because we are divine image-bearers. In spite of the fact that any particular thing is subject to change, decay, and even abuse, it is a piece of the whole and therefore has "integrity." By "integrity" we mean it is "real"; matter and its formations are not illusions of our minds. Everything has a right to exist because God either made it or created the matter out of which things are conceived and made. Therefore everything has a place in connection with everything else. The biblical way of expressing this is very simple: when God made the universe with all of its interconnecting parts, he pronounced it "good." The universe is like a wonderful pie. Its pieces all fit together into a perfect circle.

But there is more to this. Everything in the created order is "good" not only because God made it just the way he wanted it, nor is it "good" merely in the sense that we might admire and devour a fine piece of cherry pie. "Goodness" has a theological value easily missed in our society that has long considered material things as mere objects to be scientifically analyzed. To the Hebrew mind, creation was "good" because God himself is intimate with it. Isaiah falls helplessly amazed before the Lord of Hosts whose glory fills the whole earth (6:3). Jeremiah is struck by the fact that God is not a God afar off, but very near, in fact, so near that he fills all things (23:23–24). When the Psalmist repeatedly proclaims that "the earth is the Lord's and all its fullness" (24:1; 50:12; and 89:11), something more is meant than mere ownership. God is intimate with creation, so much so that his glory, something of himself, lies just beneath the surface of all material things. St. Paul picks up on this, further revealing that it is in Jesus Christ that "all things consist" (Col 1:17). Creation is good because it is charged with God's glory.

What a radical truth about our environment! The human mind has a hard time reconciling this truth with the seemingly opposite fact that God is above and beyond creation. But embracing these opposites is more of a matter of worship than of mere intellectual comprehension. Consider the awe of the psalmist as he declares how God relates to his creation:

> O Lord my God, You are very great:
> You are clothed with honor and majesty,
> Who cover Yourself with light as with a garment,
> Who stretch out the heavens like a curtain.
> He lays the beams of His upper chambers in the waters,
> Who makes the clouds His chariot,
> Who walks on the wings of the wind,
> Who makes his angels spirits,
> His ministers a flame of fire (Ps 104:1–4, NKJV)

Here God's greatness is not described in terms of how far above and beyond creation he is but, rather, how close he is. God clothes himself with light, the heavens are like his tent, foundation beams support the upper chamber upon which he is enthroned above the watery deep, the clouds are his chariots, and he walks on the wind. The pagan saw and felt these same things and out of ignorance and rebellion concluded that nature itself is divine (Rom 1:18–32). For the Hebrew, nature was not God, but he wore it like his clothes.

Let us go back to our pie imagery and see if it can take us deeper. We said above that all creation is like a pie and each piece represents a particular thing, be it a bird, fish, or a cow. Now each piece has one critical thing in common: they all come together at the very center of the pie. It is here we can envision Christ to be, at the very source or essence of every created thing, upholding all things (Col 1:17). The unity of this world can be explained by the fact that Christ is the very mysterious presence at the center of everything that has form or shape. The pie piece, here let us say, a tree, is not God, but is separate from its creator, having its own integrity of being. On the other hand, it is God who fills everything, giving it being and/or life. What is more, since God cannot be divided, the incomprehensible and unavoidable conclusion is that the whole of God possesses every piece of the pie. A piece of God cannot be here and another piece there. God is pure simple being filling the whole of his creation. In other words, everything in creation, even the smallest of things such as the ant, is "heavy" with God. The word for glory in the Hebrew, in fact, means "heavy."

Granted, this is complex philosophy, but the general idea is clear. God is intimate with every particle of creation, every piece of the pie. The universe in all of its vastness and smallness, unity and variedness, is the personal expression of God. This explains the general amazement among the prophets and disciples, let alone Jesus himself, at how dull the human soul is to the obvious. Not to see this is a form of treason, not only against God, but against ourselves. Our souls were created with a natural draw to God intimately revealed to us in our material environment. It is unnatural to be blind to this. This also explains why God takes it personally when those who refuse to see the world for what it is prefer to live in a world of their own making. It is not just a mental mistake but a spiritual and moral one also.

Nature, in all of its multifaceted intricacies, radiates God's personality. The mountains, trees, flowers, billowing seas, starry nights, moss among the trees, and the faint chirp of a cricket in autumn evenings, all reveal something about God, for all things originate in his "mind." Even scary things like lions, tigers, and bears, and as we shall see later, things dark and sad, display deep designs of divine thought. He is speaking to us through our senses. How exciting it is to see the material world as God's vast playground, a frontier of divine discovery. If we are not dumbfounded in wonder and awe, we are not seeing things as they are. We must rouse ourselves, with God's help, from the evil spell cast upon our culture by the spirit of this age that reduces everything down to mere "matter"—mere "things" to use and possess. The world and its fullness is all very holy— a temple, a cathedral, intended for an intimate encounter between God and his creatures.

5

The Cave and the Dragon

*Dragons 101: The following is a short list
of the basic characteristics of dragons.*

1. Dragons are hybrid monsters of great strength. They
   have the characteristics of bat and snake, with the
   added feature of breathing out fire, which suggests
   their infernal origin. As hybrids, they are not natural
   to creation, for God made everything in the beginning
   to reproduce after its own kind. The very idea of mix-
   ture is chaotic and unlawful.

2. Dragons live in stony caves or ancient ruins, dark and
   musty. These caves or ruins are symbolic of something
   within each of us, the crypt mentioned in chapter 3.
   The dragon loves to hide deep in the shadows or in the
   vast interior pools in the chambers of the soul. However, they are restless by nature and stir when hungry
   or provoked, creating a ruckus within and without.

3. Dragons feed on anything human. Spiritual by nature,
   they grow by dominating and devouring human spirit
   and soul; thus the human host grows weaker, or less
   human, as the dragon grows stronger. Dragons are

always associated with beautiful women either dominated or imprisoned, symbolic of the human soul held
captive. The dragon in one person seeks to feed on and
dominate other persons as well.

4. Dragons are very greedy and covetous; they hoard
treasures. Though they are incapable of spending or
enjoying their wealth, they can account for every cent,
protecting it with violence, and sleeping, as it were,
with eyes opened. These treasures are ill-gotten gains
of robbery, stolen from the human soul originally endowed with the riches God bequeathed to it.

Dragon lore has captured the imagination of our culture through the media, but it is profoundly misunderstood.
The fundamental problem is that dragons are not mere
brutes of fanciful legend, but are real—they actually exist!
The very fact that our culture is so fascinated with dragons
suggests that they are more than mere fantasy, representing
something true to our human experience.

The dragon is very old. It can even be argued that the
book of Genesis begins with one. "Now the serpent was
more cunning than any beast of the field which the Lord
God had made" (3:1, NKJV). The word translated "serpent" here obviously assumes something more than a mere
reptile in that it speaks fluently, is considered "wiser" than
other beasts, and is, therefore, categorically different in the
animal kingdom before the curse. The verbal form of the
root of this word "serpent" means "to practice magic" or
"cast a spell," and even if there is no direct etymological link
between the noun and verb, the association of this snake
with the occult is natural to the text. Surely the snake is an
agent of chaos and is intent on undermining God's good
purposes for creation.

We do not know what this snake looked like. We do know that God made it, and therefore it was not the hybrid snake/bat dragon as we know it today, for God originally made everything to reproduce after its own kind. It is not even clear how it became evil; surely God did not create it so, for Scripture will not ascribe the origin of evil to God. We can only speculate that this once very sublime creature of the field became possessed by a spiritual personality, a demon if you will, with dark intentions. As such, this creature might be considered a sort of "prototype" of what would come to be known as the chaos monster, that "twisting serpent" (Isa 27:1) often associated with the watery deep, the symbol of death. This in turn morphed into the dragon, that great hybrid monster called Satan, as we find it in the book of Revelation.

However we may speculate on this creature, what concerns us now is the interaction between the serpent and our first parents and the final result. The narrative beginning in Genesis chapter 2 verse 25, "and they were both *naked*, the man and his wife, and were not ashamed," and ending in chapter 3 verse 7, "and they knew they were *naked . . .*" is bound by the idea of nakedness (Hebrew: *ʿārûmmîm*). This idea is more profound than merely the lack of clothes, but it infers a certain transparency of personhood, innocence, lack of deceit, and integrity of character, as well as the glorious union of body and soul. This is in direct contrast to the serpent, who is said to be "crafty" (Hebrew: *ʿārûm*). This word is an obvious pun on the word "naked," a word that sounds like it but means very much the opposite. Everything that Adam and Eve were in their original state is contrasted with the serpent who was sinister, opaque, and deceitful.

What happened to Adam and Eve in their fall is complex, and it is not within the scope of this little book to examine it thoroughly. However, one thing can reasonably be inferred from the text. They took on the characteristics of the serpent through embracing its word over God's word. Before they were transparent and innocent; now they, like the serpent, were opaque and of dubious integrity. It is as if the serpent planted something in their hearts through his deceitful words. Of course, we are speaking metaphorically here, but for the sake of a vivid image that can help us understand our humanity from a certain angle, let us say that the serpent planted a seed (we will call it a "dragon seed") into the hearts of our first parents, and through them, into the hearts of all humanity.

When using this metaphor, we need to be clear here that this seed is not natural to humanity. What is essentially true about every human being is that he or she bears the image of God, even though we as a race have fallen from our original glory. The image of God is natural to us, and this is why we human beings generally carry within ourselves certain high expectations about how things should be and are shocked by evil and injustice. The dragon birthed within us from this seed is a foreign invader. However, this leaves us with a great interior struggle. The image of God within us that is reborn through our union with Christ wrestles with the dragon, which we associate here with the "old man" imagery used by St. Paul (Rom 6). This dragon dwells deep within the subterranean recesses and oceans of our vast interiors. We all walk about with our very own underworld, a veritable crypt of decay, deceit, and decadence, complete with its own monster. In fact, our soul and its conflict between good and evil is a mirror, or a world-in-miniature, of the cosmic conflict between good and evil that we see unfolding outside and around us.

Let us pick up on one astonishing implication of this imagery. Our dragons, born, raised, and to some extent nurtured within us, are like Satan who implanted the seed from the beginning—purely evil. It may be that dragons differ in some respects from person to person, but who could ever know this? What we can know is that one person's dragon is not more evil than another's, for they are all dismally evil to the same degree. I would like to flatter myself with the thought that my dragon is less offensive than, let's say, Adolf Hitler's, that famous "whipping boy" of the modern world and paragon of evil, but it is not. Hitler's dragon was merely given more opportunity than mine to wreak havoc in the world. No, my dragon is not merely potentially evil, but is the very essence of evil, evil itself. It is to the same degree evil as all the evil I see around and about me in this world. It cannot be converted; it is not redeemable. It is nasty and vicious. Someone once asked G. K. Chesterton what was wrong with the world. He answered, "Myself." Chesterton understood his dragon and how it was absolutely one with the evils of this world. You see, we are responsible for our dragons, and although dragon seed is originally foreign to us, our dragons are very much meshed into who we are, and on a profound level, are we ourselves.

Satan, that old dragon, stands at the portals of our souls and awaits opportunity. His desire is to connect with his offspring, the dragon within. He communicates to it through our senses, calling it, as it were, to stir it up from its lair to trouble the waters below. Our dragon will obediently respond. It is hell-bent on taking over and destroying that which is good in us. It hides deep within, masterly leaving the impression to our consciousness that it is not there or at least that it is tamed within. Deceit is its game; its grand aim is to take and devour. Like a parasite or a cancer, it will feed on its host until there is nothing left, and then it will self-destruct.

In our culture Dracula has taken over the medieval dragon that symbolizes pure, heartless evil. Vampires and dragons are essentially the same. They both are hybrids, both feed on humans, both are associated with beautiful women, and both are powerful and have worldly wealth. We can learn a lot of theology by watching vampire films. They are our culture's way of imaging something invisible and all too real within and without. We go through the paces of our day and we feel the presence of evil stalking us in the shadows, but we are often not quite clearly conscious of it. We all know what is feels like for others to feed on us; what we might not so readily see is that we feed on others too. This is all dragon play. What is truly frightening is that in the old movies, vampires in the end would inevitably be defeated, but since the 1960s we find that we cannot kill our monsters, and even more recently, we embrace the monster as a natural friend, "one of us" to make love with. Our culture has gone from hope, to despair, making love with its monsters.

6

The Knight and the Journey into the Interior

The fair princess and her knight rode their steeds hard with grim determination. They were approaching her home country where a dragon had spoiled the land and trapped her parents in a tower. As soon as they spied this tower, they were met with an earth-shaking roar, unnatural in its fury and evil intent, which sent a chill into the very depths of their bones. Immediately, the knight knew what he had to do; he split off to meet his fate, and she moved to a hill to behold the contest.

He was not prepared to see what was before him. The dragon was of terrific size, boasting a thick muscular body clad in metallic scales perfectly patterned, and its immense wings, unfolded and flapping like sails, sent forth ear-splitting concussions into the air. The knight found himself gazing into two blazing red reptilian eyes, but more frightful yet, knowing eyes: shining eyes that knew his secrets. Rearing its awful head, it charged him, half flying and half running full speed, with a long, snake-like tail sweeping behind it that ended in two deadly sharp stingers. The monstrosity sported huge claws razor-sharp, and its jaws opened to three rows of iron-like teeth, fetid with the gore of its victims. Sulfuric smoke of unspeakable stench belched forth from its maw, and deep within its throat, strange fire lit from the infernal regions.

Quaking with fear, the knight lifted his spear and spurred his horse to meet the charge. At impact, the spear merely glanced off, and the dragon swung its tail around and knocked horse and rider to the ground. The dragon raged when it saw the knight and his horse get up, for though the spear had failed to penetrate, it felt the knight's power. They squared off again, and this time the knight managed to pierce the creature under its wing. Letting out a shrill cry, it tore the shaft out with its claw and black, gory blood gushed out. The monster hurled its tail about and coiled around the horse, lifting the mounted knight into the air. The knight unsheathed his sword and struck the scaly crest multiple times, but it could not even dent the dragon's armor. At this point, the dragon breathed forth its fire, making the knight's armor an oven within which he baked. Seeing the knight as good as dead, the dragon threw him to the ground in contempt.

It was now getting on late in the day, and the princess from afar fell into deep sorrow over the fall of her knight. All that she could do was to pray the night through. Unknown to her, at the place where her knight fell was a spring with life-reviving virtues for both body and soul that had survived the dragon's wasting of the land. These marvelous waters worked healing into the knight, and in the morning he arose refreshed and ready for battle. He attacked the dragon, landing a blow to its head with his blade that also seemed to have benefitted from those mysterious waters, leaving a

deep gash. The dragon let out a roar of such a hor-
rific magnitude that trees were overthrown and
rocks split asunder. It took to the air and dived
down upon the knight, thrusting one of its stingers
through the knight's shield and penetrating into
his shoulder. In rage, the knight managed to hew
the tail of the dragon off in five places, leaving but
a stump.

The dragon bellowed smoke into the air so as
to darken the sun and, without a tail, clumsily
charged the knight, grabbing his shield with its
claw. They fought back and forth, but finally
the knight chopped off the claw that hideously
remained clamped onto the shield. At this, the
dragon belched forth fiery bile of hellish magma,
forcing the knight to stagger back, fainting from
the heat, suffocating in the smoke, and sickened
by the bile. When all seemed lost, the knight fell
back upon a tree loaded with fruit most perfect
and rare. Unclean things cannot endure the purity
of this tree, so the dragon stood back, glowering in
pain, fear, and hatred. Night again fell, and the
princess took to prayer, anxiously waiting what
the morning would bring.

The fruit of this tree revived the knight. In the
morning he went out again against the dragon,
which now was determined to devour him. The
knight, however, took advantage of the opened
mouth and thrust his sword deep into the head,
causing a mortal wound. The dragon collapsed
with an awful earth-shaking crash, and the victo-
rious knight looked upon the deformed mass before him in shock and amazement. The princess,
when she saw that the monster was indeed dead,
drew near, praising God, and thanking her knight.

THIS KNIGHT AND DRAGON story is from Edmund Spenser's *Fairie Queene*, written in what C. S. Lewis called the "Golden Period" of English literature when the nation was both deeply aware of and appreciative of the old myths that formed England's national consciousness. To us this story may seem corny; we are more interested in how realistic we can make our cinematic dragons and how we can depict the action. The Elizabethans, however, were more interested in the symbolism. It was not just a story; it taught them who they were, about the reality of the world in which they lived, and what was required of them.

To begin with, everyone, if they want to find out the truth about themselves, must resolve to make a journey into their interior. Moreover, one cannot make the journey on one's own; not only does one need a guide, but no one is prepared for, or capable of, facing the terrors that lurk within. Spenser would have us understand that Christ is the knight and the princess is the soul. The three day battle is fought and won by Christ who descended into the netherworld for three days, defeating death and Satan. The soul's responsibility is to pray like the princess without ceasing.

From another perspective, the knight and the princess can be seen as two aspects of the human soul traveling together with Christ, the ever-present but invisible guide who manifests himself at critical times through mysterious springs and trees, symbolizing the graces of baptism and communion. We are all feminine—a princess destined to a kingdom and to union with Christ the King. We are also knights, and we must wage war with our dragon. The dragon is too horrible to describe, fierce and powerful, with weapons and armor that we could never hope to stand up to in our own natural strength. But face it we must, for if we do not defeat it, the dragon will surely devour us. Dragons do not go away easily. The battle is a horrible, messy, and bloody thing, but if we have resolve, pray, and take advantage of the graces Christ provides, we can and will prevail.

It is clear that our Christian culture has lost the knowledge that underlies these metaphors. We no longer think in terms of interior journeys, battles, and an evil presence lying deep within our subterranean chambers. Our theology is shallow; we live in the "sunny side" where Jesus paid it all and have no true grasp of the work that we must do together with Jesus to fulfill our identity and destiny. More likely than not, we have some sense of the infernal regions of our interiors, but we ignore them, and out of fear, subconsciously attempt to stabilize our psyche by negotiating a peace treaty with the monster. But the monster knows no peace. It knows that we have no stomach for the fight, and over a long period of time it can get us to compromise ever so slightly on many different occasions. It is patient and persistent; it wants to lay claim to our interior universe, making it a wasteland, a reflection of itself.

The history of Israel provides a vivid example of this sorry process. God miraculously delivered Israel from Egypt and provided leadership through Joshua to take the land of Canaan. With God fighting for them, the Israelites swiftly took overall control of the land; it was theirs! Yet there were Canaanites still in the land with which they had to deal in order to make their possession complete. They failed, and in very little time they became Canaanites themselves. The same holds true with Christians. Christ has won the war on the cross; we are a new creation in him. Yet we, like Israel, must engage in battle with our "old man," putting it to death, lest we inadvertently feed it, and it grows into a dragon that will bring us to ruin. There is no other way; we must fight to live. "What becomes really ours is what we fight for inch by inch, killing as we go; slaughtering the obstinate foe on his own soil, so that the property be left to us uncontested."[1]

But how does one go about this journey? First and foremost, we need to get to the point where we are convinced that we do have a vast interior region within, a territory to be conquered, an enemy to face. Only then will our determination harden, our passions begin to stir, and our anger become focused. You must notice the grim determination of our knight and the anger needed in the heat of the battle. Then, we must be convinced that we are not alone, that Christ is with us, and that God's grace leads us all the way. We grow restless with a holy restlessness. Through much prayer and self-knowledge, plans begin to formulate, preparations begin, faith grows, and we find ourselves going out the front door with walking stick in hand. We are speaking, of course, of a journey unlike any other that we have experienced. It doesn't necessarily have a specific point or time of departure nor involve a physical relocation; those around us may not even sense that we are on our way.

This is all very spiritual and mustical, so let us go back to our map room where we began in order to get a handle on what this journey is about. Those who plan journeys into unknown regions pour over maps and books. They read what others have experienced and said about their trip and the battle. This is critical, for if we can gain a sense that others have gone before, and that it is, in fact, possible to conquer our dragon, our imaginations become engaged in the enterprise and hope is kindled. There are those who speak with authority; we call them spiritual directors because of their knowledge of the human interior. St. John of the Cross is a classic example. Consider these lines from his poem "The Living Flame." We get a sense that this man has

1. Dodds, *Israel's Iron Age*, 18.

been there and that the journey is possible and that we can succeed by the grace of God.

> O lamps of fire bright burning
> With splendid brilliance, turning
> Deep caverns of my soul to pools of light!
> Once shadowed, dim, unknowing,
> Now their strange new-found glowing
> Gives warmth and radiance for my Love's delight.[2]

All journeys into our interior frontiers are different because God created us as unique individuals. However, the general structure of the soul and its mission is the same for us all. There are those who have gone before, and they can show us the way. The very fact that St. John of the Cross can speak of dark caverns once lying in the unknown shadowy depths now turned to pools of light, sends a thrill of joy and hope into the inquiring soul!

Let us say one last word on the dragon. Again, we are speaking in a metaphor here. The metaphor is used only to visualize to our consciousness, something that, due to its spiritual nature, is beyond our ability to completely comprehend with our minds. Moreover, we need to embrace a paradox here about the Christian life. On one hand, we are a new creature in Christ; the "old Adam" part of us has been crucified with Christ and no longer defines who we are. We are to reckon ourselves dead to sin from which we have been set free (Rom 6). On the other hand, the old nature, of which the dragon imagery is a part, is never completely dead and is still a factor in our lives with which we must deal, not in our own strength, but in the power of God. St. Paul uses violent military metaphors to describe this reality (e.g., Gal. 6:10–18; Col 3:5–10) that is in line with what has been said above about the dragon. "Putting off" the old

2. In Matthew, *The Impact of God*, 24.

man and "putting on" the new man is a dynamic endeavor that continues throughout our lives (Eph 4:17–24), for the dragon is ever hungry, and there is always the irrational impulse within us to feed it. Though the dragon stays with us in this life, by the power of Christ we can attack it, starve it, and beat it into submission.

All of this is done in prayer. Notice that the princess' only action in the story above is prayer. We might say that setting out on the journey into the interior is a metaphor for the intentional resolve to live a life of prayer. Surely prayer is at times deep communion with God and a great comfort, but we see, however, that prayer is not always a warm and cozy place to be. Rather, it is in prayer that we meet the devil, just as Jesus met the devil during his forty-day fast and later in Gethsemane. Prayer is where Jesus himself, though divine and sinless, grew in power against the powers of darkness, culminating in his resolve to sacrifice himself totally. We are to do what he did, and we can do it because he is with us. And so prayer is the battleground where we face the dragon within and the devil without. It is hard, the hardest thing we humans can do. But all great endeavors are hard, demanding perseverance, patience, commitment, and much practice. This is why so few really live the life of prayer.

7

The Super Bowl

I confess that I have a competitive nature. I hate this about myself. Therefore, I try my best to avoid games and situations where this unbecoming trait flairs up. Recently, however, my two children have become football fans, and I, in order to relate with them, got sucked into it. You see, we live in Baltimore, and the Ravens' arch foe is the Pittsburgh Steelers. There may be no greater rivalry in pro football. It is amazing to me how this competition can grip the soul. One's very identity gets caught up with the team: when the Ravens do well, we are happy for a week, raving over every great play: when they lose, we hang our heads for days in the agony of defeat. This is very painful for me, for I strive to have a recollected soul, and when my energy is dissipated by temporal things that have little or no eternal value, I know that I am failing myself and God.

YET COMPETITIVENESS IS WOVEN into the very fabric of human nature. We are endlessly fascinated with any contest of mind, strength, will, and skill. As for football, it culminates in what has become in America the greatest of all sporting events, the Super Bowl. Tickets for this event are precious, and the whole country and, yes, much of the world, is riveted to their television sets. We may even suggest that it takes on a religious fervor; it is a sacred moment in which we forget ourselves and abandon our usual constraints, yelling and cheering on our team.

There is something more to this than meets the eye: every game is a symbol of deeper realities. It is in the context of the great stadium, the vast crowd of spectators, and the titanic struggle for victory that we find our next frontier. The battle with our dragon and the devil, though presented in the last chapter as a private matter, is really no private matter at all. It is all fought before a multitude of witnesses. For a typical westerner, whose reality is his own individuality and what he sorts out with his reason, observation, and experience, this is completely foreign ground. We might *think* that we think like the early Christians, but in reality we live in two different worlds. In our experience, at least for many of us, there is a huge wall separating us from this world and the spirit realm; the dead have nothing to do with us, nor do we have anything to do with them.

In Hebrews 12:1 we are informed of a crowd of witnesses viewing our contest; they consist of rows and rows of champions of previous generations who have fought the good fight and succeeded. Many of these were martyrs. What was so new to the world was the Christian understanding of the dead. Those who died in Christ were not considered to be dead but more alive than they were in their mortal flesh. Only this belief explains their willingness and even expectation that they would die for the faith. Moreover, the heaven they inhabited was not cut off from this world but was intrinsically linked to it. A martyr did not only die before a vast crowd of Roman pagans but before a greater and more wonderful crowd, an illustrious multitude of just persons make perfect: the saints.

This heavenly arena is not without order. In fact, every saint is perfectly situated in his or her proper place. Moreover, the early Christians understood that angels also, all according to their ranks, fill the celestial stadium in a multitude too numerous to count. This reality was revealed to St. Paul, who tells us of thrones, dominions, principalities, and powers (Col 1:16), and who was caught up into the third heaven (2 Cor 12:2ff.). Whatever this means, there is a realm just beyond our senses that is so real that, in contrast, what we experience here in this physical world, in this body, is very dark and shadowy indeed.

What is truly difficult for so many of us in today's world to grasp is that this vast crowd of witnesses, both glorified saints and angels, is not merely watching and cheering, but is actively participating in our contest and our struggles. Angels were created along with the world and are inseparable from it. Even we, when we pass on to the spirit world, do not leave this world behind only to be enthralled in some sort of ecstatic vision that renders us ineffectual in the created order. The spirit realm as presented to us in Scripture is not passive but highly active, and it is necessarily linked to this world. Every being made by God, especially angelic and human, was made with integrity and purpose, and God works his grace in us on earth through a heavenly hierarchy of intermediaries. God's kingdom is one of order consisting of beings endowed with real power.

We can readily agree that Christ is the great intermediary between God and humanity. However, Christ is the great king, who empowers his heavenly court to do his bidding. He could do everything directly himself, but then he would not be respecting his creatures that he has created to accomplish critical tasks in heaven and earth. It is understood that God works his grace to us through persons he brings into our lives, either directly or indirectly. The early

Christians did not believe that death discontinued this flow of grace to us. In fact, death intensified this power to help us, for in death, especially a martyr's death, one is purified and empowered to help all the more. In our culture, we do not hesitate to ask someone to pray for us. For many, however, it does not seem natural to ask those who have passed on into the spirit world to petition for God's help. This hesitancy has little or nothing to do with Scripture. Rather, it has to do with a worldview deeply influenced by secular Western ideas that will not admit to any real link between the kingdom of God and this earth.

This chapter is not meant specifically to be an apologetic for the praying to and asking intercession from saints and angels. There is no doubt that there have been abuses when Christ the king has become so remote and distant that some no longer feel connected to Jesus, but turn to the saints instead. Rather, this chapter is meant to address the opposite problem in which one believes that there is no longer any meaningful link between us and the spirit world of saints and angels. In the Bible, these two have been made one in Christ, and there is now no barrier between them. There is but one church consisting of all.

Perhaps we can here meld together our images of the cathedral and the Super Bowl. Cathedrals have what is called a clerestory high above the nave, the area where the congregation sits. Consisting of rows of windows, the clerestory opens up the cathedral to the heavens. We might go further and envision the crowd of celestial witnesses assembled around, about, and above us in the clerestory, deeply intent on us, interceding, and endowing us with gifts and graces from Jesus. This is reality. We must either live in this reality to be whole or choose to live in a truncated world with no windows opening up to heaven. The choice here is no small one. How we conceive our world has great spiritual and moral implications.

The fight of our life, the contest for our very souls, is not fought in lonely isolation, though the devil would have us think so. We have Jesus and his whole kingdom at our disposal. Heaven is bent over us, engrossed with every move, every play, and every choice. The Super Bowl is but a superficial representation of the real thing. Here competition is at its supreme height, for the stakes are high. Every soul, no matter how obscure in this world, is known among heaven's throngs the way football players are known to the fans. The future of the world hangs upon every contest; nothing and no one is small in the scheme of things. This, I think, is why we are so fascinated with sporting competitions, because we all know deep down in our heart of hearts that we are in a great contest ourselves, although we might not be overtly conscious of this fact.

Let us see ourselves on a quest, a quest to discover reality as it really is, not as it has been handed to us by our culture. We have the power through Christ and his church to explore all regions, all worlds, not only that which is within but also that which is above. Yes, heaven itself with its celestial choirs is a frontier that we can familiarize ourselves with here and now.

Finally, it is a strange irony that football is played on Sundays, the Lord's day. In the book of Revelation, Sunday was the context for worship (1:10), and this worship is specifically described in chapter 4. We see heaven open, hear the invitation to come up, view the great throne and the twenty-four elders (representing the Old Testament and New Testament saints) around the throne, hear the Sanctus sung, and participate in this holy worship. Like the journey into our interiors, this pilgrimage to heaven is made through prayer and especially through the Lord's Supper, where all of God's children—those on earth and those in heaven—join together and dine with their Lord. To discover corporate worship around the Eucharist is to experience union between heaven and earth.

8

The Leper Colony

When Fr. Damien was ordained, he understood his call to mean that he was to die to self and enter into the sufferings of Christ. He considered himself a dead man walking. The place of his labors was pleasant enough; he was a missionary in Hawaii! By the 1870s, however, a terrible and strange disease introduced by the trading ships had spread throughout the islands—leprosy! The Hawaiians did not know what to do with their lepers, so they shipped them to an island named Molokai, and isolated them on a piece of land that lay between the mountains and the beach. There they were expected to fend for themselves, which, of course, they could not do. It was a colony of unimaginable horror whose members decomposed while yet alive. They did not even have the will or energy to bury their dead. In spite of the breathtaking scenery, the blue waters and the pounding surf, the sunshine and the breeze in the trees, nothing could be closer to hell on earth. For those torn from their families and shipped forever away, Dante's famous line in his Inferno *was most applicable: "Abandon all hope you who enter here!"*

Faced with the dilemma of serving these lepers, the bishop asked for volunteers, fully aware that it was a death sentence. Fr. Damien accepted without hesitation, knowing that this was his destiny. Upon landing on the beach, he was greeted by his new parish. What he saw was suffering beyond comprehension: people whose extremities were missing or in the process of rotting, faces without noses, hollow eye sockets filled with maggots, and what was especially frightful were young children with swollen faces and enlarged ears, looking like gnomes from a fantasy world, experiencing pain as no child should! His first priestly act was to give last rights to a young man in a primitive straw hut. He was lying in his own putrid mess; Fr. Damien, not used to the stench, had to go outside for fresh air. When he went to anoint the feet, he thought he saw them moving in the dim light. The legs and feet were dead; what was in motion was the mass of crawling vermin.

From the first, Fr. Damien made a resolution to himself that he would not shy away from his people but live with them in a most human way— touching, embracing, and cleaning wounds. This, along with organizing the lepers, building permanent houses and buildings, creating burial details, and doing services, filled his days from dawn to dusk. In the evening after his meager supper, he would share his pipe with his leper friends. Damien knew that it was only a matter of time before he would succumb to the disease. God gave him about ten years before this happened, but even before he contracted leprosy, he lived as a leper among the lepers. Fr. Damien came to serve, suffer, and die.

It is amazing how these lepers responded to Fr. Damien. He gave them a sense of dignity and hope. After a few years when he became famous, some curious visitors came to visit Molokai. One of them remarked about how the lepers loved music. The organist had but one hand, and that with two fingers left. With the stub of the other he managed to fasten a stick by which he struck the bass notes. Once the visitor saw a musician lose a part of his finger and a section of his lip fell off in the middle of the piece, but he kept on playing with passion. These lepers had music in their hearts.

THE WORLD WE LIVE in now is very much afraid of suffering. Since Voltaire lost faith in the face of the tragic Lisbon earthquake in the mid-eighteenth century, rejecting with contempt the idea that this is the best of all possible worlds, and that suffering has its place, the Western world has had grave trouble reconciling how there could be a good God in a world with leper colonies. We find ourselves stumped with this dilemma, and in the end, we tend to distance ourselves from God and do what we can to avoid suffering. This is a very natural reaction for us in our culture of plenty, ease, and science. However, Fr. Damien saw something that is not easy for modern eyes to see. He saw that suffering was a path into a frontier where one discovers rare beauties not found elsewhere. In fact, it was among the dead that he found life.

It is here also that we see the world as it is. Fr. Damien exemplifies Christ. Jesus came into the world that was for him very much like a leper colony. Like Damien, he came to serve, suffer, and die. The lepers recognized and respected Fr. Damien because he became one of them. We, the lepers, if we are humble enough to see ourselves as we really are, recognize and embrace Jesus because he became one of us.

This explains Jesus' enduring hold on the human soul; he became a leper like us, and so there is a basis for mutual understanding between the divine and the human. Suffering is the bridge. We cross it and we discover Christ, and in Christ all the secrets of the world are waiting to be revealed to us.

This leads us back to chapter 4 and our image of the pie. There we brought up the idea that Christ was intimate with every "piece of the pie," that is, everything in creation. We can readily understand that this divine intimacy shows itself in all that is beautiful and pleasing. However, there is no escape from the logic that if Christ is intimate with everything, then he must also be intimate with all that is unseemly, nasty, and ugly. Moreover, he is not only intimate with things on earth but also with the motion of things as they unfold in time. This means that Jesus is intimate with all the sorrows of space and time to the point where we can say that all suffering is divine suffering.

The implications of this are truly astounding. We are completely wired to assume that the pain and suffering we experience is, in fact, our private burden. If we are Christians, we gain some comfort knowing that Christ is suffering with us. However, the opposite is true. When we suffer, we are really entering into divine suffering, because, in a sense, all suffering is God's suffering. Christ's mystical intimacy with creation cannot be separated from his incarnation. The cross is the meeting place in space and time where all sin, pain, suffering, and loss meet. His sufferings are completely different from ours in that Jesus' suffering must be understood as whole and complete, embracing the totality of human history, whereas ours, no matter how terrible, is only part of the whole. All suffering is divine suffering in which we participate.

This brings us back to Fr. Damien. Because he had a profound grasp of divine suffering, he lost his fear of it. In fact, he saw it as a means of becoming one with Christ as St. Paul did in Philippians when he confesses his great desire to know Jesus and the fellowship of his sufferings, being conformed to his death (3:10). Suffering now becomes a pathway into a frontier that opens up to God. It is here where we see the heart of God, comprehend what he is like, and experience his love and power in the midst of what humans by nature consider weakness and hopelessness. Ask the lepers who came to love Fr. Damien; there in Molokai they found the true meaning of life, true joy, and divine secrets that most of those on the outside never find.

9

The Big Splash

Are there not, dear Michal,
Two points in the adventure of a diver?
One, when, a beggar, he prepares to plunge,
One, when, a prince, he rises with his pearl?
Festus, I plunge.[1]

—Browning, "Paracelsus," part 1

THERE IS SOMETHING PRIMAL about the sea. It is always calling me, like the distant rumble of thunder, the dancing flames in the fireplace, or the wind rushing through the pines. Living as we do by the Atlantic Ocean, we rarely miss our annual pilgrimage to the shore. Part of our family ritual is to read poetry, a favorite being Wordsworth's "The Secret of the Sea:"

    ... Till his soul was full of longing,
       And he cried, with impulse strong,—
    "Helmsman! For the love of Heaven,
       Teach me, too, that wondrous song!"

---

1. In Sencourt, *Carmelite and Poet*, 107.

> "Wouldst thou"—so the helmsman answered,
>   "Learn the secret of the sea?
> Only those who brave its dangers
>   Comprehend its mysteries!"[2]

I love to spend hours on the beach where the waters meet the sand. The constant pounding of the waves after some time makes its way into the soul, washing away temporal cares. The eye takes in the vast expanse of sea and sky as the mighty breakers crash in perfect formation. The sunlight sparkles on the retreating water, creating multitudes of diamonds on the rippled sand.

Personally, I do not like the process of getting out into the water. Off the Delaware and Maryland coasts, the ocean is cold—at least I think so! Unlike my son who bravely runs out to meet the waves, I inch my torturous way into the churning watery chaos until, battered, I take the final plunge. Once the sea rolls over me, I find it a refreshing experience. In the depths of my soul I feel alive in a very different way than on land. A small dot at the edge of oceanic mystery, my soul tests itself against unfathomable power and depths,

> Till my soul is full of longing
>   For the secret of the sea,
> And the heart of the great ocean
>   Sends a thrilling pulse through me.[3]

The biblical world saw the watery deep as one of the primal elements of chaos, along with darkness and the formless earth. As such, it was a symbol of death. To pass through the waters is to pass through death to something beyond, whether it is Noah's flood, the Red Sea, the Jordan

2. In Untermeyer, *The Golden Treasury of Poetry*, 261.
3. Ibid.

River, or the waters of baptism. Death is the big splash that awaits us all. That sea does not give up its dead; no mortal that enters comes back.

Of course there were ancient myths that spoke of those who, like Osiris, Hercules, Persephone, and Aeneas, crossed the river of death and came back again. But these were the gods, demigods, or literary fabrications—exceptions to ordinary mortals. Moreover, they never could alter the nature of the underworld; it stood inexorably fixed as a place of eternal gloom—a monster with open maw waiting for its inevitable victims. Of course there were the Elysian Fields, or heaven, but this was reserved only for the elite few; the common herd of humanity had little or no hope of ever attaining the bliss for which every human heart naturally longs.

The fact that Christ was believed to have entered hell at his death and "take captivity captive" by freeing the underworld of its prisoners is fundamental to the way Christians through the ages understand reality. Though the idea of the journey to the underworld is as old as humanity, this was a radical shift of worldview. Here was a historical man who many knew intimately, revealed to them as God incarnate, who sacrificed himself to death for the express purpose of blasting through the gates of the underworld, plunging through the waters of death, and claiming the realm of the dead for himself. His ultimate triumph was that he returned—something that had never happened before! The ramifications of this were stupendous to those who first fully realized what had happened! Death no longer held any power over them! It lost its sting!

The most fundamental doctrine of Christianity is that the church and each of its members are in union with Christ. This is ultimately a mystery that the mind cannot comprehend. However, St. Paul explains it by way of contrast; before we were "in Adam" and whatever was true about Adam was true about us, especially sin and death. Now, we are in Christ, and what is true about Christ is now true about us. We have been baptized into Christ, and by virtue of our passing through the waters of baptism, it is as if we, too, made the journey that Christ made, and possess a stamped passport, as it were. The underworld as it was once feared is no longer our fate; indeed, it is no longer real to us. In baptism we died to all that could hold us in death.

What binds us in union with Christ is the love by which Christ sacrificed himself for us on the cross. This love draws us into the strangest metamorphosis of all! Love now becomes the very frontier of death. By daily taking up our cross and dying to ourselves out of love for God and humanity, death and love become one. To explore the regions of love is to explore the regions of death. When Father Damien entered the realm of the dead at the leper colony, he entered the frontier of love that opened up to him treasures beyond the borders of what we humans, in our natural state, hold onto as "life." When it came time for him to die physically, it was absolutely of no consequence to him, for he was already dead to self. God's lovers are the walking dead.

Peter Kreeft, in his excellent book *Love is Stronger than Death*, provides five metaphors to help us make our way to this mysterious marriage of death and love. The first two are death as enemy and death as a stranger. By nature we cannot help but view death as an enemy in that it is not original to creation but was imposed upon it by sin. This is supported by the fact that death is universally abhorred by all. Death is therefore viewed, in all the old myths as well as in many places in the Old Testament, as a devouring monster. If this is the metaphor through which we ultimately see death, then we cannot help but despair. In today's culture it is also common to view death as a stranger, an "it" objectified as a scientific fact of nature. This is supported by the pornographic way death is cheaply dealt out in the media, obscenely displaying the dead. We stare at "it," but do not know what "it" is. In reality, death is *us*, for by definition we are mortals—death creatures—and we are every minute of our lives dying, now! To treat death as a stranger, as a scientific or cinema graphic "it," is to be estranged from ourselves.

The next three metaphors work in sequence, moving from death as a friend, as to a mother, and finally as a lover. Since death is us, we must become acquainted with ourselves. It takes courage and openness to make friends, especially one as frightening as death. But when we think about it, death frames our life like a picture; it sets our life in relief and enables us to appreciate life as the gift it really is. Death teaches us to love, and without death there would be no self-sacrifice, no noble deeds, nor courage. We admire, for instance, Fr. Damien, for the very fact that he befriended death by his noble acts, and by doing so, befriended himself and humanity.

Kreeft goes on to tell us that once death is seen as a friend, then we can see it as a mother. A mother is, among many things, the door of life. As a mother births us into this world, so death births us into spiritual worlds. To discover any of the frontiers discussed in this book is a birthing, or from another perspective, is a death. When we grasp death as friend and mother, we are then left to make the ultimate choice: to make death our lover. This is not meant in a morbid way! Death is an evil and must not be glorified! However, God uses death, the ultimate horror of life, as the ultimate means of union with him! Consider these lines penned by one of the greatest lovers in the church, St. John of the Cross:

Ah bring thy presence nigher,
And kill me with thy aspect and thy grace!
Love is ordeal by fire,
Torment too fierce and dire
    To cure, but by thy presence and thy face.[4]

You will notice that the mystic associates God's presence with death itself, for to see God, all that is mortal in us must die. Kreeft tells us that prayer itself is death's rehearsal, for in prayer we come intentionally to God as lover, and each time we do, we suffer a "little death."[5]

We all have a rendezvous with the sea; it is calling us! Many there are that live in dread of it, ignoring its call. If they go to the beach, these people will miss the "secret of the sea," preferring the warmth of the sun and sand, thinking how nice they will look with a tan. It is lost on them that the sea is indeed a frontier that we are equipped, by the power of the resurrected Christ, to explore here in this life. Like all adventures, the hardest part is at the beginning. Some hearty-souled folk, like St. John of the Cross or Father Damien, dive right in and make the big splash all at once. There are many, like me, who hesitate along the edge, only slowly testing the waters and with a wary eye calculating the waves, getting used to the ocean at intervals as it makes its torturous way up the torso until we find the courage to plunge or are pummeled underneath a breaker. It is then we discover that the love of Christ empowers us to subsist underwater, and that which is death becomes life to us. "Only those who brave its dangers comprehend its mysteries," and rise with the pearl.

---

4. "The Spiritual Canticle," stanza 11 in Senecourt, *Carmelite and Poet*, 96.

5. Kreeft, *Love is Stronger than Death*, 104.

Conclusion

HERE I STAND IN my map room. High above me is a good, all-powerful God that fills eternity, and it will take eternity even to begin to discover all the wonders of his glory. Beneath him the heavenly spheres are lined, row upon row, with angels and saints bent over in rapt attention to what God has set in motion on the earth here displayed on my fantastic map. Before me is a world that radiates with the very presence and glory of Christ in all of its parts. I look inside and see that there is a universe within me, of vast spiritual space, a reflection of the universe above me and the world about me built like a cathedral complete with clerestories and ribbed vaulting, and stained glass windows through which divine light beams down upon the altar of my soul. Deep within there is the crypt where the dragon lies, submerged in my deep subterranean underworld. I must go down and meet it with my champion knight, Jesus Christ. Danger is everywhere; the devil and evil spirits desperately desire to connect with my dragon within and destroy me. Angels and saints intercede for me in my struggle. Suffering is everywhere, but Christ, whose cross stands in the center of all space and time, is the ultimate sufferer; all suffering is essentially his, for he fills all things, and gives all things meaning. I look in the mirror and see the traces of death in my aging face. I lose a loved one. I am not afraid nor will I despair, for death as enemy and stranger has been defeated and has been transformed by love into a friend, mother, and lover.

This is the cosmos as presented in the Bible. It is an enchanted place, consisting of worlds within worlds; like Ezekiel's divine chariot, each of its four wheels is a wheel within a wheel, and all four wheels move in complete harmony because the same Spirit is in them all. So, too, with our cosmos. In our little book we have presented six worlds that we have called frontiers. We venture into one and find that it is a door to the others. They are perfectly designed to fit together, like Russian dolls. God is the great artist, and when we begin to see, really see, the magnitude of the spheres within, around, and above us, we fall to our knees in awe and worship.

But how do we begin to find our way into these realms? Our natural spiritual sluggishness is greatly aided by a culture that has intentionally shut its doors to the frontiers presented in this book. First, we have to understand that it is God who desires us to be adventurers, and that he is beckoning us all the time. He has imbedded within us a natural curiosity and desire to discover the truth about him, about ourselves, and about the world in which he has placed us. We have to appropriate this desire and learn how to see, hear, and think all over again.

The frontier with which we naturally begin is the physical realm, for our senses are most immediate to us. From infancy up to puberty, we humans see and sense everything around us with the freshness of first-time wonder. We sense more than just mere "objects"; our first discovery of nature is intensely spiritual, and the wonder of it all is, in fact, the wonder of God. This is how we all know God intuitively. As we grow, this pristine wonder is eventually lost, and the connection between the physical realm and the spiritual realm tends to breaks down in us. Nature for most of us, at least in our day and age, must be a frontier to be rediscovered. William Blake—the great English poet, artist, and mystic who lived at the very beginning of the Industrial Age and the onset of materialism—observed that "The tree which moves some to tears of joy is in the eyes of others only a green thing that stands in the way."[1] To this we add Abraham Heschel's poignant statement: "He who thinks that we can see the same object twice has never seen."[2]

Surely this is what Jesus means when he tells us that we must become like little children to enter into the kingdom of God. Humility does not come quickly. For most of us it gradually dawns, and with it illumination slowly makes its way into our hardened souls. At first it comes in little flashes, in our most unguarded moments, always a surprise, when our hearts are not consumed with worries or inane thoughts; sometimes it comes through the most common things, such as a crack in a rock. The flash of joy is the joy of God, an encounter with Jesus who upholds all things, a breakthrough into another dimension.

At some point we become curious about ourselves. How is it that I have certain powers to connect so deeply with all that is around me? How and why do I have these magnificent endowments of memory and imagination? So much of my past lies stored within my soul, and my mind can take me anywhere I have been and wherever I want to be. I find that I love and that love expands within me to seemingly limitless dimensions. Ah, this must be con-nected to Jesus' cryptic statement that the kingdom of God is within! Within me is a virtual universe, a place of vast spiritual space, a cathedral worthy of God. Jesus invites me to come in, explore, and play! I find that there is a world

1. In Ackroyd, *Blake: A Biography*, 209.
2. Heschel, *The Prophets*, 1:12.

within that reflects the world without and that the world within can even contain the world without.

But all of this is not in isolation. If this is true about me, then surely it is true about my brothers and sisters around me. How can I think of other humans as common or incidental when they too possess such treasures? As a Christian I am part of a great organism called the church, intimately connected with all the saints who have gone before me—all part of a tapestry of time and space—with whom I have the power of "mystic sweet communion." Angels, who approach the edges of the created spiritual sphere, the fiery servants of God, are part of the very fabric of our reality whether we feel present to them or not. All of this is ours, frontiers for us to explore. As we discover ourselves, we discover others, discover other realms, and discover God who is above and beyond all.

As we discover ourselves and others, we cannot help but venture into the realms of suffering and death. We are sufferers, and we are death. In what we naturally fear as a chamber of horrors, we are most surprised to find instead the treasures of darkness. Behind the black shrouds we see Christ enthroned, for he has defeated the monsters within and without. Love's power, not very evident in the minds of natural humanity, now displays itself in full color. What we thought was pain and death is love, and love is pain and death.

Everything and everywhere are interwoven. All the frontiers within and without are before us. To discover one is to discover all. In the end they all take us to God who is above and beyond everything and everywhere. Jesus encourages us to ask, seek, and knock. Knock on the doors that open up to these frontiers with your longing hearts— pray and study, study and pray. Do not lose heart, do not let your passions stray and disperse. We are not mere water bugs scuttling on the surface of cold and dark December waters. We are divine image bearers, designed to search out wild and wonderful frontiers, and it is our duty in this benighted age to rediscover the lost realms once so familiar to our Christian ancestors.

Postscript

Why It Is So Hard for Us to See

IF WHAT YOU HAVE read in this little book seems new and strange, there is a reason for this. A spirit of darkness has benighted our culture, and it has made deep inroads even into the church. We believe that we are thinking biblically about our world but in reality we are not. Nothing could be clearer about Scripture than that it presents us with a world of mystery, spiritual powers, supernatural encounters of various kinds, miracles, and a realm charged with the glory of God. If we are honest about ourselves, that picture of the world is alien to many of us. We have been given a set of lenses by the so-called "Enlightenment" of the eighteenth century through which we, along with our culture, look at our world. They have, to a great extent, robbed us of the supernatural. Let us briefly consider six of these lenses that distort our vision.

The first of these lenses is a critical spirit. We are taught to doubt everything that we cannot verify by our senses and reason and anything that we have not experienced personally as real. This locks us up into the small world of our own thoughts. It matters not that we are true believers in Jesus, that we have had an authentic encounter with Jesus, and that our lives have been dramatically changed. Conversion can happen quickly, but change in our essential worldview is another matter. We are still "modern," or if you will, "postmodern" westerners, and what makes us what we are is a spirit that is critical of anything that goes beyond our senses, comprehension, and experience. By nature we associate credulity with naivety, and doubt is embraced in the depths of our hearts as a virtue, a sign of intelligence. True, critical thinking has a bright side and has brought many wonderful advances in our world. However, it also has a dark side that, if we are not aware of it, will darken the soul to spiritual realities.

Closely associated with this critical spirit is the lens of autonomy. We interpret freedom not as the power to choose what is right and true, but as our own personal right to think and act the way we want to without regard to any real authority. Again, this locks us up in our own private world. If we do not like what one particular preacher or church tells us, we simple move on to another one. When we listen to any teaching, we tend to judge it not with the biblical text in light of two thousand years of church history, but according to whether we think it is right or not. Usually this is highly selective and based on personal feeling that is rooted not, as we think, in the Bible, but in the sentiments of our culture. The result is that we are really operating on our own; we are alone in a cultural sea of lonely people. The spirit of autonomy separates us from the frontiers that we have discussed in this book, for to penetrate into them demands that we are thoroughly dependent on the roadmaps that the church has left us over the centuries.

The third lens is that of "practicality." In a culture that bows down to scientific and technological breakthroughs and has a passion for immediate, concrete results in the physical world, most of what is said in this book is simply not "practical." Results in the spiritual realm, however, occur in a far different way than those in factories and laboratories.

Persons who set out on spiritual quests often have little to show for it, at least at first, and are roundly condemned as being "too heavenly-minded to be of any earthly good." We fail to understand the deep connection between hours and years of silent, unseen spiritual striving and the profound countercultural breakthrough of the kingdom of God. The result is that the demon of the practical has created a plastic, superficial culture that has no tools at all to penetrate into the spiritual realities within and around us.

The next two lenses, relativity and tolerance, combine to undermine true spiritual insight. The world has become a small place bringing into conflict many diverse worldviews and beliefs. The pressure to get along necessitates, in the secular mind of the culture, the doctrine that all things spiritual are relative, and that there is no universal truth that can apply to all. In this way of thinking, belief in universal truth inevitably leads to violence. The realms described in this book are considered mere metaphysical speculation, which, if it works for you, is fine, but has no application to the whole of humanity. However, what we really have are worlds in conflict: a secular worldview that has no categories for spiritual realities versus the historical church that founds its worldview on Scripture. Christ, through the church, has the authority and the means to speak wisdom to the world. Tolerance is good and essential, but its dark side is religious indifference. Indifference paralyzes the pioneering spirit, and relativity undermines the drive to discover the truth about God, humanity, and creation.

The last lens is that of an eclectic attitude with regard to how we function intellectually and spiritually in our environment. Because of the fragmentation created by the lenses described above, we cannot see how the whole of reality fits together. We are left with bits and pieces of various competing and contrasting worldviews, and we pick and choose elements here and there to create a collage that simply does not make sense when we stand back and take a hard look at it. We paste various ideas from Scripture together with modern ideas of freedom, individualism, and materialism. Given our temperaments, we either live in our heads, dominated by doubt and critical thinking, or we live through our emotions and feelings. We are taught by our culture that our reason does not apply to spiritual things, that it is impossible for the whole of reality, life and death, the spiritual and the physical, joy and suffering, inside and outside, or heaven and earth to fit together. Therefore, we do the best we can to survive, even as Christians, with incredible anxieties birthed by deep-lying inconsistencies in our worldview.

The whole point of this little book is that we do not have to live this way. If we can do the brave work of questioning the lenses through which we look, we will no doubt see how much our thinking is culturally conditioned. When this happens, a longing to know what is real and true is fostered, and we strike out on a spiritual journey. Of course, this book is too short to be a comprehensive guide into all the frontiers introduced in it. All it can do is open up the possibilities, thus stimulating our curiosity to venture out and explore. As we give ourselves over to the quest for these holy realms largely lost to us moderns, slowly we will find ourselves less fragmented and becoming more and more whole and integrated.

Bibliography

Ackroyd, Peter. *Blake: A Biography.* New York: Knopf, 1996.

Dods, Marcus. *Israel's Iron Age, Or Sketches from the Period of the Judges.* New York: Hodder & Stoughton, n.d.

Gay, Peter. *The Enlightenment: An Interpretation.* New York: Norton, 1977.

Heschel, Abraham J. *The Prophets.* Vol. 1. New York: Harper, 1962.

John of the Cross, Saint. *The Collected Works of St. John of the Cross.* Translated by Kieran Kavanaugh and Otilio Rodriguez. Washington, DC: Institute of Carmelite Studies, 1991.

Kreeft, Peter. *Love is Stronger than Death.* San Francisco: Ignatius, 1992.

Lewis, C. S. *English Literature in the Sixteenth Century.* Oxford: Clarendon, 1954.

Matthew, Iain. *The Impact of God: Soundings from St. John of the Cross.* London: Hodder & Stoughton, 1995.

Origen. *Homilies on Leviticus: 1–16.* Translated by Gary Wayne Barkley. Washington, DC: The Catholic University of America Press, 1990.

Sencourt, Robert. *Carmelite and Poet: A Framed Portrait of St. John of the Cross.* New York: MacMillan, 1944.

Underhill, Evelyn. *Mysticism.* New York: Image, 1990.

Untermeyer, Louis, ed. *The Golden Treasury of Poetry.* New York: Golden, 1959.

Made in the U
Monee, IL
23 January 2020